Ben P

A TENDER THING

adapted from William Shakespeare's
Romeo and Juliet

NICK HERN BOOKS

London

www.nickhernbooks.co.uk

ROYAL
SHAKESPEARE
COMPANY

ABOUT THE ROYAL SHAKESPEARE COMPANY

The Royal Shakespeare Company at Stratford-upon-Avon was formed in 1960 as a home for Shakespeare's plays, classics and new plays.

The first Artistic Director Peter Hall created an ensemble theatre company of mostly young actors and writers. The core of the work was Shakespeare, combined with a search for writers who were as true to their time as Shakespeare was to his. The Company was led by Hall, Peter Brook and Michel Saint-Denis. Hall's founding principles were threefold. He wanted the Company to embrace the freedom and power of Shakespeare's work, to train and develop young actors and directors and to experiment in new ways of making theatre. Rejecting dogma, he urged the company in a 1963 address to "Keep open, keep critical... Our Company is young, we are searching, and whatever we find today, a new search will be necessary tomorrow."

The Company has had a distinct personality from the beginning. The search for new forms of writing and directing was led by Peter Brook. He pushed writers to experiment. "Just as Picasso set out to capture a larger slice of the truth by painting a face with several eyes and noses, Shakespeare, knowing that man is living his everyday life and at the same time is living intensely in the invisible world of his thoughts and feelings, developed a method through which we can see at one and the same time the look on a man's face and the vibrations of his brain."

A rich and varied range of writers flowed into the company and have continued to do so with the RSC's renewed commitment to placing living dramatists at the heart of the Company. These include: Harold Pinter, Howard Barker, Edward Bond, Howard Brenton, Edward Albee, David Edgar, Peter Flannery, Martin Crimp, Caryl Churchill, Tony Harrison, Wole Soyinka, Stephen Poliakoff, Tom Stoppard, Timberlake Wertenbaker, Martin McDonagh, Marina Carr, debbie tucker green, David Greig, Rona Munro, Adriano Shaplin, Roy Williams and Anthony Neilson.

Alongside the Royal Shakespeare Theatre, the Other Place was established in 1975. The 400-seat Swan Theatre was added in 1986. The RSC's spaces have seen some of the most epic, challenging and era-defining theatre – Peter Brook's Beckettian *King Lear* with Paul Scofield in the title role, Charles Marowitz's *Theatre of Cruelty* season which premiered Peter Weiss' *Marat/Sade*, Trevor Nunn's studio *Macbeth*, Michael Boyd's restoration of ensemble with *The Histories Cycle* and David Greig's and Roy Williams' searing war plays *The American Pilot* and *Days of Significance*.

The Company today is led by Michael Boyd, who is taking the Company's founding ideals forward. His belief in ensemble theatre making, internationalism, in new work and active approaches to Shakespeare in the classroom has inspired the Company to landmark projects such as *The Complete Works Festival, Stand up for Shakespeare* and *The Histories Cycle*. He is overseeing the transformation of our theatres which will welcome the world's theatre artists onto our stages to celebrate the power and freedom of Shakespeare's work and the wealth of inspiration it offers to living playwrights.

The RSC Ensemble is generously supported by
THE GATSBY CHARITABLE FOUNDATION and THE KOVNER FOUNDATION

The RSC Literary Department is generously supported by THE DRUE HEINZ TRUST

The RSC's New Work is generously supported by
CHRISTOPHER SETON ABELE on behalf of THE ARGOSY FOUNDATION

The 2009 Newcastle Season is assisted by a grant from
THE NORTHERN ROCK FOUNDATION

The RSC is grateful for the significant support of its principal funder,
Arts Council England, without which our work would not be possible.
Around 50 per cent of the RSC's income is self-generated from Box Office sales,
sponsorship, donations, enterprise and partnerships with other organisations.

Supported by
**ARTS COUNCIL
ENGLAND**

This production of *A Tender Thing* was first performed by the
Royal Shakespeare Company at Northern Stage, on 29 October 2009.
The cast was as follows:

ROMEO	**Forbes Masson**
JULIET	**Kathryn Hunter**

Directed by	**Helena Kaut-Howson**
Designed by	**Neil Murray**
Lighting designed by	**Vince Herbert**
Music by	**John Woolf**
Video designed by	**Jacques Collin**
Sound designed by	**Mike Compton**
Movement by	**Lucy Cullingford**
Company Dramaturg	**Jeanie O'Hare**
Company text and voice work by	**Jacquie Crago**
Assistant Director	**Michael Fentiman**
Music Director	**Laurie Perkins**
Casting by	**Hannah Miller** CDG
Production Manager	**Rebecca Watts**
Costume Supervisor	**Christopher Cahill**
Company Manager	**Michael Dembowicz**
Stage Manager	**Suzanne Bourke**
Deputy Stage Manager	**Juliette Taylor**

MUSICIANS

Violin	**Bethan Morgan**
Cello	**Elaine Ackers**
Piano	**Laurie Perkins**

EMBEDDED WRITERS AT THE RSC

The potential for new work at the RSC is something we take very seriously. Our embedded writer policy is just one of a raft of strategies designed to inspire playwrights.

We believe that a writer embedded with our actors helps establish a creative culture within the Company which both inspires new work and creates an ever more urgent sense of enquiry into the classics. The benefits work both ways. Actors naturally learn the language of dramaturgical intervention and sharpen their interpretation of roles. Writers benefit from re-discovering the stagecraft and theatre skills that have been lost over time. They regain the knack of writing roles for leading actors. They become hungry to put death, beauty and metaphor back on stage.

As part of this strategy we have played host to key international writers for the last three years. Tarell McCraney is our current RSC/CAPITAL Centre International Playwright in Residence. He works in the rehearsal room with the Ensemble Company on our Shakespeare productions. Whilst contributing creatively to the work of the directors and actors he is also developing his own writing and theatre practice. His new play for the RSC will be performed by this current Ensemble in 2011. His post is funded by the CAPITAL Centre at Warwick University where he teaches as part of his residency.

Tarell follows on from Adriano Shaplin who was with the RSC from 2006-8.

We also invite British writers to spend time with us in the rehearsal room and contribute dramaturgically to both our main stage Shakespeares and our Young People's Shakespeare. There is a generation of playwrights who are ready to write their career-defining work. We are creating conditions at the heart of the RSC in which this generation can take themselves seriously as dramatists and thrive.

THE RSC IN NEWCASTLE

There have always been three points to the RSC triangle: Stratford, London and Newcastle. Our companies have always loved playing to Newcastle audiences. This year we return to perform in three of the city's most exciting theatre spaces: Live Theatre, Northern Stage and The Theatre Royal. We are also collaborating on a raft of projects with local performers, writers and directors; in theatres, schools, universities and quay sides.

Newcastle has been home to many great playwrights and many great plays have been written here. It is thrilling to open the world premiere of *A Tender Thing* in a city with such a long and distinguished cultural legacy. It is fantastic that 2009's residency in Newcastle truly represents the range of RSC work: major productions of Shakespeare plays, two significant new plays, *The Comedy of Errors* in schools, a reading of *The Castle* by Howard Barker as part of an international celebration, as well as an opportunity for audiences and artists to meet in pre- and post-show events, workshops and a symposium. And alongside all this we're seeding local projects we hope will blossom and grow over the next few years. With the RSC now committed to an increased output of new work, one of the projects we're most excited about is working with five emerging playwrights at Live Theatre as they tour the city looking for the inspiration that will turn their new play into tomorrow's masterpiece.

For more details of what's on in Newcastle visit our website: **www.rsc.org.uk**

Roxana Silbert
Associate Director

THE COMPANY

JACQUES COLLIN
VIDEO DESIGNER

RSC DEBUT SEASON:
A Tender Thing.

theatre includes: From 1990 – 2009 Jacques has worked as a multi-media designer for Robert Lepage's production company, Ex Machina. Productions include: *Lipsynch, 1984, Le Moulin à Images, The Andersen Project, Dragon's Trilogy, La Casa Azul/Apasionada, The Far Side of the Moon, Métissage, Jean-Sans-Nom, Geometry of Miracles, Elsinore, The Seven Streams of the River Ota, Needles and Opium.*

other work includes: *UKIUK* (National Capital Commission, Ottawa); *Constantinople* (Gryphon Trio, Toronto/Banff Arts Center/ Royal Opera House); *Le Clan des Oiseaux, Mahler's 8th Symphony* (Quebec Symphony Orchestra); *Northern Light – Visions and Dreams* (Veronica Tennant Productions/CBC).

MIKE COMPTON
SOUND DESIGNER

RSC: Mike is Senior Sound Technician for the RSC.
this season: *A Tender Thing.*
theatre includes: Before joining the RSC Sound Department 6 years ago Mike worked for a number of the country's leading theatres

and production companies, including The Almeida, Donmar Warehouse, National Theatre and the RSC both nationally and internationally.

LUCY CULLINGFORD
MOVEMENT DIRECTOR

RSC: Lucy has worked as a movement practitioner within the RSC Movement Department since 2007. *A Midsummer Nights Dream, The Winter's Tale* (RSC Youth Ensemble).
this season: *A Tender Thing.*
theatre includes: *The Bear/The Proposal* (C Company. Bridewell Theatre); *Spoonface Steinberg* (UK tour); *Stoopud Fucken Animals* (Traverse); *Magic to Cry For* (Resolution. The Place); *A Small Family Business, Wuthering Heights* (West Yorkshire Playhouse); *Grace Online, No Stone Unturned, Missing Melanie* (Youth Music Theatre UK); *Mikey the Pikey* (Pleasance); *Moby Dick, Bouncers* (West End); *Pigs, Big Trouble in the Little Bedroom, Thick as a Brick* (Hull Truck Theatre); *The Dumping of the Snark* (Lawrence Batley); *Mother Goose, Aladdin, Treasure Island, Alice in Boogie Wonderland* (Everyman Theatre); *ON Song, Quartet for the End of Time* (Opera North).

other: Lucy has taught at ALRA, Mountview Academy of Theatre Arts, Arts Educational, Rose Bruford and for the RSC Education Department.

MICHAEL FENTIMAN
ASSISTANT DIRECTOR

RSC DEBUT SEASON: *As You Like It, A Tender Thing.*
trained: Michael trained as an actor at Bretton Hall and later as a Director at Mountview Academy.
theatre includes: Directing: *Spoonface Steinberg* (Clwyd/ Greenwhich/Glasgow Citizens/tour); *Blue/Orange* (Cockpit); *Guy* (Pleasance), *East* (Basingstoke/tour); and he has been developing *Lady Of Sorrows* with Little Angel Theatre. Michael was previously Associate Director at the Playhouse Theatre in Harlow. Credits include: *Romeo and Juliet* (professional cast merged with a large community chorus), *The Wizard of Oz* and numerous Christmas pantomimes. He has been Assistant Director to Tim Baker (Theatre Clwyd), John David and John Adams (Basingstoke Haymarket) and Marina Calderone, on a number of productions.
other credits include: *Ajax* (Cyprus tour), *Richard III, Messiah: Scenes from a Crucifixion, The Dumb Waiter, Bouncers.*

Michael is currently Artistic Director of Beggars and Kings.

VINCE HERBERT
LIGHTING DESIGNER

RSC: Vince is currently Head of Lighting for the RSC. *Hamlet, Twelfth Night.*
this season: *A Tender Thing.*
other theatre includes:
West End: *The Accused, Lady Windermere's Fan* (Haymarket); *Animal Crackers* (Lyceum); *Blood Brothers* (Phoenix). Repertory: *Tender* (Hampstead); *Vertigo, The Importance of Being Earnest* (Theatre Royal, Windsor); *Carmen* (New Victoria); *Abigail's Party* (Nuffield); *Animal Crackers* (Royal Exchange/Barbican); *Romeo and Juliet* (Belgrade); *Blood Brothers* (national tour); *American Bagpipes, Amongst Barbarians, The Odd Couple, She Stoops to Conquer, Blithe Spirit, The Miser, The Moonstone, The Brothers Karamaazov, Maybe, The Count of Monte Cristo, Look Back in Anger, Private Lives, Miss Julie, Hindle Wakes, The Philadelphia Story, The Candidate, Peer Gynt* (Royal Exchange); *Cinderella* (Vienna); *Mother Tongue* (Greenwich); *Il Seraglio* (Scottish Opera); *Acis and Galatea* (Manchester Cathedral).

KATHRYN HUNTER

JULIET

RSC: Artistic Associate. *Othello* (as director), *Everyman* (RSC/BAM, New York).
this season: Gavrilo in *The Grain Store*, Juliet in *A Tender Thing.*
work as a performer includes: *Fragments* (Young Vic/Bouffes du Nord/world tour); *The Bee* (Soho); *The Maids* (Brighton Festival); *Yerma* (Arcola); *Celestina* (Birmingham/Edinburgh Festival); *Whistling Psyche* (Almeida); *Richard III* (Shakespeare's Globe); *The Taming of the Shrew, Dona Rosita* (Almeida); *King Lear* (Leicester Haymarket/Tokyo Globe); *Macbeth, Electra* (Leicester Haymarket); *Far Away* (Bouffes du Nord); *The Rose Tattoo, The Devils* (Theatr Clwyd); *Live Like Pigs, The Recruiting Officer, Our Country's Good* (Royal Court); *Pericles, The Visit* (Olivier Award for Best Actress. National Theatre). Theatre de Complicite includes: *Foe, Help, I'm Alive!, The Winter's Tale.*
work as a director includes: *4.48 Psychosis* (LAMDA); *The Birds* (National Theatre); *Destination* (Volcano Theatre Co.); *Wiseguy Scapino* (Theatr Clwyd); *Mr Puntila and his Man Matti* (Almeida/Albery/Traverse); *The Glory of Living* (Royal Court); *The Comedy of Errors, Pericles* (Shakespeare's Globe).
film and television includes: *Harry Potter and the Order of the Phoenix, All or Nothing, Wet and Dry, Orlando, Baby of Macon, Rome, Silent Witness.*

HELENA KAUT-HOWSON
DIRECTOR

RSC DEBUT SEASON: *A Tender Thing.*
trained: Polish Academy of Theatre in Warsaw and RADA in London.
theatre includes: *Marat/Sade, Little Foxes, Another Country* (Leeds Playhouse); *Tess* (West Yorkshire Playhouse), *Henry IV Part 2, Henry V, Amadeus* (Octagon Bolton); *Small Family Business* (Birmingham Rep); *Vassa* (Greenwich Theatre/Centaur Theatre, Montreal); *Boesman and Lena, Cat's Play, Alpha Beta, A Doll's House, Dusa Fish Stas & Vi* (Habimah National Theatre of Israel); *Hagoel* (Jerusalem Theatre); *Remembrance, Top Girls* (Cameri Theatre, Israel);

The Plough and Stars, The House of Bernarda Alba, Spokesong (Lyric, Belfast); *Jane Eyre* (Gate, Dublin); *Werewolves* (TDM Montreal/ Druid Theatre, Galloway) . From 1991 to 1995 Helena was Artistic Director of Theatr Clwyd, Wales. Work included: *The Devils* (Liverpool Post Award for Best Production), *All's Well that End's Well, Jane Eyre* (Playhouse, London), *Full Moon* (international tour/ Young Vic), *Macbeth, The Rose Tattoo* (Best Director 1995 TMA Regional Theatre Awards). Since leaving Clwyd Helena's productions include: *Major Barbara* (Shaw Festival, Canada); *The Seagull, Summerfolk* (NTS Montreal); *Sweet Bird of Youth* (Haifa Theatre,Israel); *All's Well that End's Well* (Regent's Park); *King Lear* (Leicester Haymarket/Young Vic/Tokyo Globe); *Hindle Wakes* (MEN Best Production Award); *The Taming of the Shrew, Mrs Warren's Profession, Much Ado about Nothing* (MEN award), *Marriage of Figaro, The Miser* (Royal Exchange); *Yerma* (Arcola), *Victory* (Grand Prix for the Best Director at the 2003 Festival of Premieres. Wroclaw Wspolczesny Theatre, Poland); *Measure for Measure* (Krakow Slowacki Theatre, Poland); *Spring Awakening* (Warsaw Powszechny Theatre, Poland).

opera includes: *Maskarade and the Duenna* (Opera North); *Die Fledermaus* (Opera Dolnoslaska, Poland); *Koanga* (Sadler's Wells).

FORBES MASSON

ROMEO
RSC: *The Histories Cycle, Twelfth Night, The Comedy of Errors, Macbeth, Hamlet, The Pilate Workshop.*
this season: Jaques in *As You Like It*, Samson in *The Grain Store*, Romeo in *A Tender Thing.*
trained: RSAMD.
theatre includes: *King Lear* (Liverpool Everyman/Young Vic); *The Breathing House, Art, Much Ado about Nothing* (Lyceum, Edinburgh); *San Diego, Dumbstruck, Cinzano, Endgame* (Tron); *A Wee Bit of How Do You Do, Sounds of Progress, The Trick is to Keep Breathing* (Tron/Toronto/Royal Court); *The Real World* (Tron/ New York); *Laurel and Hardy* (Edinburgh/New Zealand); *The Life of Stuff* (Donmar).
television includes: *No Holds Bard, EastEnders, The High Life, Hamish Macbeth, Red Dwarf.*

radio includes: *McLevy, Forbes Masson Half Hour, The Trick is to Keep Breathing, Conan Doyle – A Life in Letters.*
writing includes: *Stiff!, Mince?* (also directed. Nominated for Best Musical, TMA Awards 2001), *Pants* (also directed).
Forbes is an Associate Artist of The National Theatre of Scotland.

NEIL MURRAY
DESIGNER
RSC DEBUT SEASON:
A Tender Thing.
Neil is Associate Director and Designer at Northern Stage.
theatre at Northern Stage includes: *The Threepenny Opera, Carmen, They Shoot Horses Don't They?, Therese Raquin, The Tiger's Bride, The Bloody Chamber, Pandora's Box* (co-directed with Emma Rice), *Great Expectations, Kaput* and numerous Christmas shows. He has also designed much of the company's earlier work including: *A Clockwork Orange, 1984, Wings of Desire, Animal Farm, Blood Wedding, Twelfth Night, Romeo and Juliet.*
other theatre includes: *1001 Nights Now, Wings of Desire* (Betty Nansen Theatre, Copenhagen); *The Princess and the Goblin, Laurel and Hardy, Mrs Warren's Profession* (co-produced

with Nottingham Playhouse); *Vanity Fair, Mary Rose, Copenhagen, Confessions of a Justified Sinner* (Royal Lyceum, Edinburgh); *The Gymnast* (Jane Arnfield at Edinburgh Festival); *Brief Encounter* (Evening Standard award for Best Design, Critics Circle award for Best Design, nominated for whatsonstage. com award and Olivier award for Best Design. Kneehigh at Cinema Haymarket/UK tour/ USA tour).

Neil's work is presented in the design books *Make Space, Time Space* and *Collaborators*. His design for *Homage to Catalonia* was selected for inclusion in the UK National Exhibition at the Prague Quadrennial of Scenography 2007, which was subsequently shown at the Victoria and Albert Museum.

BEN POWER WRITER

RSC: *The Tempest, Much Ado about Nothing* (Complete Works Festival). **this season:** *A Tender Thing.* Ben has worked as dramaturg for companies including Complicite and Shakespeare's Globe. He is Associate Director of Headlong Theatre, acting as dramaturg and literary manager on all productions.

theatre includes: *Adolf Hitler: My Part in his Downfall* (Rho Delta/Watford Palace); *The Things She Sees* (National Theatre, New Connections); *Cinderella* (Lyric Hammersmith/Warwick Arts Centre); *Six Characters in Search of an Author* (Headlong/Chichester/ Gielgud); *A Disappearing Number* (Evening Standard Award for Best Play, Critics' Circle Award for Best New Play, Laurence Olivier Award for Best New Play. Complicite/Barbican/ international tour); *Faustus* (Headlong/Hampstead/ UK tour); *Paradise Lost* (Headlong/Hackney Empire/ UK tour; *Tamburlaine the Great* (Rose Theatre).

radio includes: *A Disappearing Number.*

LAURIE PERKINS MUSIC DIRECTOR

RSC DEBUT SEASON: *A Tender Thing.*

trained: University of Bristol, Guildhall School of Music and Drama.

theatre includes: As Conductor and Associate/ Assistant Music Director: *Carousel* (Savoy); *The Lord of the Rings* (Drury Lane). As Music Director: *The King and I* (UK tour); *Only You Can Save Mankind* (Edinburgh);

two *Musical Futures* showcases (Greenwich); *Showtime* (Venue); *City of Angels* (Guildhall); and a string of Sondheim musicals at Mountview Academy of Theatre Arts. Other productions Laurie has been involved in include: *Avenue Q* (Noël Coward/ Gielgud); *Jersey Boys* (Prince Edward); *La Cage Aux Folles* (Playhouse); *Wicked* (Apollo Victoria); *Oliver!* (Drury Lane); *The Phantom of the Opera* (Her Majesty's); *Hello Dolly!* (Regent's Park); *West Side Story* (UK tour); *Billy Elliot* (Victoria Palace); *Mary Poppins* (Prince Edward/ UK tour); *Zorro* (Garrick); *Amadeus* (Wilton's Music Hall); *Anything Goes* (Drury Lane); *Chicago* (UK tour/ European tour/Lebanon); *A Funny Thing Happened on the Way to the Forum* (National Theatre); *Guys & Dolls* (Piccadilly/UK tour); *Hollywood Symphonic* (Lille Opera House); *Imagine This* (New London); *Into the Woods, Pinocchio, Wind in the Willows* (ROH2), *Marguerite* (Haymarket); *Side by Side by Sondheim* (Gordon Craig, Stevenage); *Sunset Boulevard* (UK tour); *Sweeney Todd* (UK tour); *Take Flight* (Menier Chocolate Factory).

television includes: *Genius, I'd Do Anything, Your Country Needs You.*

JOHN WOOLF
COMPOSER

RSC: John is RSC Head of Music. He joined the wind band in 1977, and was appointed Music Director for Stratford in 1987. Since then he has been MD on most of Shakespeare's plays and other productions including: *Fair Maid of the West* (1987 Royal opening of the Swan), *The Wizard of Oz, The Beggar's Opera, Faust, The Lion, the Witch and the Wardrobe, The Secret Garden, Beauty and the Beast*.

this season: *As You Like It, The Grain Store, A Tender Thing*.

trained: Read music at St John's, Cambridge and Royal Academy of Music, studying oboe with Janet Craxton. Winner of 1970 York Bowen Prize.

as composer/arranger work includes: *The Quest, Moliere, Twin Rivals, Measure for Measure, Seeds Under Stones, Troilus and Cressida, A Midsummer Night's Dream, Timon of Athens, Miss Julie* (West End); *The Tempest, Twelfth Night, Hamlet, The Histories Cycle*.

film: MD for Trevor Nunn's *Twelfth Night*.

Production Acknowledgments

Scenery, set painting, properties, costumes, armoury, wigs and make-up by RSC Workshops, Stratford-upon-Avon. Thanks to Professor Ammar Al-Chalabi PhDStat from King's College Motor Neurone Clinic, London. Production photographer Keith Pattison. Access performances provided by Louise Ainsley, Phillip Armstrong and Stephen Weller.

FOR THE RSC IN NEWCASTLE

Jeremy Adams
Producer

Rachael Barber
Touring Administrator

David Collins
Head of Marketing

Claire Gerrens
Senior Electrician

Fiona Keston
Wigs and Make-up Mistress

Anna Mitchelson
Marketing Manager (Productions)

Tim Owen
Specialised Senior Electrician

Andrew Playford
Specialised Senior Sound Technician

Tom Watts
Specialised Senior Stage Technician

Kevin Wimperis
Specialised Senior Stage & Props Technician

Nada Zakula
Senior Press Officer

SUPPORT THE RSC

As a registered charity the Royal Shakespeare Company relies on public support and generosity.

There are many ways you can help the RSC including joining Shakespeare's Circle, RSC Patrons, through Corporate support or by leaving a bequest.

RSC Patrons and Shakespeare's Circle

By supporting the RSC through Shakespeare's Circle and RSC Patrons you can help us to create outstanding theatre and give as many people as possible a richer and fuller understanding of Shakespeare and theatre practice. In return you receive benefits including priority booking and invitations to exclusive supporters' events. Shakespeare's Circle Membership starts at £8.50 per month.

Help Secure our Future

Legacy gifts ensure that the RSC can develop and flourish in the years to come, bringing the pleasure of theatre to future generations that you yourself have enjoyed.

Corporate Partnerships

The RSC has a national and internationally recognised brand, whilst retaining its unique positioning as a Warwickshire-based organisation. It tours more than any other UK-based arts organisation and has annual residencies in London and Newcastle upon Tyne. As such it is uniquely placed to offer corporate partnership benefits across the globe.

The Company's experienced Corporate Development team can create bespoke packages around their extensive range of classical and new work productions, education programmes and online activity. These are designed to fulfil business objectives such as building client relationships, encouraging staff retention and accessing specific segments of the RSC's audience. A prestigious programme of corporate hospitality and membership packages are also available.

For more information, please telephone **01789 403470**.

For detailed information about opportunities to support the work of the RSC visit **www.rsc.org.uk/support**

TRANSFORMING OUR
THEATRES

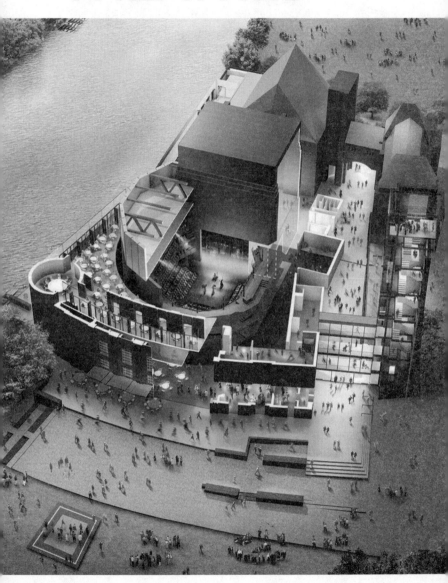

In 1932, following the 1926 fire which destroyed much of the original Shakespeare Memorial Theatre, a new proscenium arch space opened in Stratford-upon-Avon, designed by Elizabeth Scott. Now known as the Royal Shakespeare Theatre the building boasted a spacious, fan-shaped auditorium housed inside Scott's art-deco inspired designs.

And now the RST is undergoing another transformation from a proscenium stage to a one-room space allowing the epic and intimate to play side by side.

At the heart of the project will be a new auditorium. Seating around 1,000 people, the stage thrusts into the audience with theatregoers seated on three sides, bringing the actor and audience closer together for a more intimate theatre experience.

The new space will transform the existing theatre, retaining the key Art Deco elements of the building. A new Theatre Tower with viewing platform, theatre square for outdoor performances, a linking foyer to join the Royal Shakespeare and Swan Theatres together for the first time, and new public spaces are central to the new building.

7,000 people have already supported the transformation from over 40 countries worldwide. To find out more and to play your part visit **www.rsc.org.uk/appeal**

LOTTERY FUNDED

GET MORE INVOLVED

RSC Membership

Become an RSC Member and enjoy a wide range of benefits.

Full Member £36 (per year).
As an RSC Full Member you receive up to four weeks' priority booking with a dedicated hotline into the RSC Box Office, Director's selection of four exclusive production photographs per year, regular Members' newsletters, access to Members' only web pages, special ticket offers – save £20 on two top price tickets in Stratford (conditions apply) and 10% discount in RSC Shops, Mail Order, RSC Short Breaks and at The Courtyard Theatre Café Bar.

Associate Member £15 (per year).
As an RSC Associate Member you receive priority booking of up to two weeks with a dedicated hotline into the RSC Box Office, regular Members' newsletters and 10% discount in The Courtyard Theatre Café Bar and with RSC Short Breaks.

Gift Membership.
All membership levels can be bought as a gift.

Overseas Membership.
This is available for those living outside the UK.

To find out more or to join, please contact the Membership Office on **01789 403440** (Monday-Friday 9am-5pm) or visit **www.rsc.org.uk/membership**

GET MORE INVOLVED

RSC Friends

As a network of the RSC's most active supporters, RSC Friends are important advocates for the Company, encouraging people to enjoy a closer relationship with the RSC and its work on and off stage.

Joining the Friends costs £20 a year and is open to RSC Full and Associate Members. Benefits include a lively programme of events plus a quarterly Friends' Newsletter and further opportunities to become more closely involved with the RSC.

For more information or to join, please contact the Membership Office on **01789 403440** or join online at **www.rsc.org.uk/membership**

RSC Online

www.rsc.org.uk

Visit the RSC website to Select Your Own Seat and book tickets online, keep up to date with the latest news, sign up for regular email updates or simply learn more about Shakespeare in our Exploring Shakespeare section.

THE ROYAL SHAKESPEARE COMPANY

Patron
Her Majesty the Queen

President
His Royal Highness The Prince of Wales

Deputy President
Sir Geoffrey Cass

Artistic Director
Michael Boyd

Executive Director
Vikki Heywood

Board
Sir Christopher Bland (*Chairman*)
Professor Jonathan Bate FBA FRSL CBE
Michael Boyd (*Artistic Director*)
Damon Buffini
David Burbidge OBE
Jane Drabble OBE
Noma Dumezweni
Mark Foster
Gilla Harris
Vikki Heywood (*Executive Director*)
John Hornby
Jonathan Kestenbaum
Paul Morrell OBE
Tim Pigott-Smith
Neil Rami
Lady Sainsbury of Turville (*Deputy Chairman*)

The RSC was established in 1961. It is incorporated under Royal Charter and is a registered charity, number 212481.

A TENDER THING

Ben Power

Adapted from William Shakespeare's
Romeo and Juliet

For Dee

To Old Age:

I see in you the estuary that
enlarges and spreads itself
grandly as it pours in the great
Sea.

Walt Whitman

Characters

ROMEO

JULIET

This text went to press before the end of rehearsals and so may differ slightly from the play as performed.

Prologue

Darkness and music. A door and a large bed. Beyond, the sea moves gently. The door opens and an elderly man enters. He holds a small blue bottle.

ROMEO.
  Give me the light.

Lights rise. He walks over and sets the bottle down at the foot of the bed.

Thou detestable maw, thou womb of death
Gorg'd with the dearest morsel of the earth.
A grave? O no, a lantern,
For here lies Juliet and her beauty makes
This room a feasting presence, full of light.
Ha!
How oft when men are at the point of death
Have they been merry, which their keepers call
A lightning before death. O how may I
Call this a lightning? O my love, my wife,
Death that shalt suck the honey of thy breath
Hath no power yet upon thy beauty.
Thou art not conquer'd. Beauty's ensign yet
Is crimson in thy lips and in thy cheeks
And Death's pale flag is not advanced there.
Wilt thou remain so fair? Shall I believe
That unsubstantial Death is amorous,
That the lean abhorred monster shall keep
Thee here in dark to be his paramour?
For fear of that I here will stay with thee
And never from this palace of dim night
Depart again. Here, here will we remain
And worms shalt be our chambermaids. O here
Shall we set up our everlasting rest
And shake the yoke of inauspicious stars

From our world-wearied flesh. Engrossing Death!
Come, bitter conduct, come, unsavoury guide,
Thou desperate pilot now at once run on
The dashing rocks these seasick-weary barks.

In the bed, a sleeping figure wakes.

JULIET.
Good even to my ghostly confessor.
Either my eyesight fails or thou lookst pale.

ROMEO.
And trust me, love, in my eye so do you.
Is there no pity sitting in the clouds
That sees into the bottom of our grief?
Eyes, look your last. Arms, take your last embrace.
And lips…

JULIET.
Sssh.
I do remember well where we should be
And here we are. Where is my Romeo?

ROMEO.
Call me but love and I'll be new baptis'd:
Henceforth I'll never be thy Romeo.

JULIET.
Did my heart love till now? Forswear it, sight.
For I ne'er saw true beauty till this night.
Give me thy hand.

He reaches out towards her as the music swells. The couple dance as the bed fades into the distance and the sea surrounds them.

Scene One

Music and the light of a late-summer sunset floods the room.
ROMEO *is alone.*

ROMEO.
O heavy lightness! serious vanity!
Mis-shapen chaos of well-seeming forms!
Feather of lead, bright smoke, cold fire, sick health.
Why, such is love!
Love is a smoke raised with the fume of sighs,
Being purged, a fire sparkling in lovers' eyes,
Being vexed, a sea nourish'd with lovers' tears.
What is it else? a madness most discreet,
A choking gall and a preserving sweet.
I have lost myself, I am not here,
This is not Romeo, he's some other where.
There is a woman...
And for a lifetime, nay, for many lives
On her alone my heart's love has been set.
As mine on hers, so hers is set on mine,
My wife, my friend, my crutch, my soul's fair twin.
Read o'er the volume of her glorious face,
And find delight writ there with beauty's pen.
Examine every married lineament,
And see how one another lends content
And what obscured in this fair volume lies
Find written in the margent of her eyes.
It will seem strange but I have seen the day
That I have worn a visor and could tell
A whispering tale in a fair lady's ear
Such as would please. 'Tis gone, 'tis gone, 'tis gone.
But soft! What light?

JULIET *enters and he moves back against the wall.*
Believing herself to be alone, JULIET *sits.*

(*Aside.*) It is the east, and Juliet is the sun.
Arise, fair sun, and kill the envious moon,
Who is already sick and pale with grief,
That thou her maid art far more fair than she.

Be not her maid, since she is envious,
Her vestal livery is but sick and green
And none but fools do wear it, cast it off.
It is my lady, O, it is my love!
She speaks yet she says nothing – what of that?
Her eye discourses, I will answer it.
I am too bold, 'tis not to me she speaks.
Two of the fairest stars in all the heaven,
Having some business, do entreat her eyes
To twinkle in their spheres till they return.
What if her eyes were there, they in her head?
The brightness of her cheek would shame those stars,
As daylight doth a lamp. Her eyes in heaven
Would through the airy region stream so bright
That birds would sing and think it were not night.
See, how she leans her cheek upon her hand!
O, that I were a glove upon that hand,
That I might touch that cheek!

JULIET.

Gallop apace, you fiery-footed steeds,
Towards Phoebus' lodging: such a wagoner
As Phaethon would whip you to the west,
And bring in cloudy night immediately.
Spread thy close curtain, love-performing night,
That runaway's eyes may wink and Romeo
Leap to these arms, untalk'd of and unseen.
Lovers can see to do their amorous rites
By their own beauties; or, if love be blind,
It best agrees with night. Come, civil night,
Thou sober-suited matron, all in black,
Hood my ancient blood, rising in my cheeks,
With thy black mantle, till young love, grown old,
Renew itself and spring forth fresh once more.
Come, night; come, Romeo; come, thou day in night;
For thou wilt lie upon the wings of night
Whiter than new snow on a raven's back.
Come, gentle night, come, loving, black-brow'd night,
Give me my Romeo, and, when he shall die,
Take him and cut him out in little stars,
And he will make the face of heaven so fine

That all the world will be in love with night
And pay no worship to the garish sun.
O, Romeo, Romeo...

ROMEO (*aside*).

Shall I hear more, or shall I speak at this?

JULIET.

O, Romeo, so tedious is this day
As is the night before some festival
To an impatient child that hath new robes
And may not wear them.

Stepping forward, ROMEO *puts his hands over her eyes.*

ROMEO.

I take thee at thy word!
O, speak again, bright angel! for thou art
As glorious to this night, being o'er my head,
As is a winged messenger of heaven
Unto the white-upturned wondering eyes
Of mortals that fall back to gaze on him
When he bestrides the lazy-pacing clouds
And sails upon the bosom of the air.

JULIET.

If my ears had not drunk a hundred words
Of that tongue's utterance, still I'd know the sound.

She spins around and embraces him.

Thou know'st the mask of night is on my face,
Else would a maiden blush bepaint my cheek
For that which thou hast heard me speak tonight.
Fain would I dwell on form, fain, fain deny
What I have spoke: but farewell compliment!
Dost thou love me? I know thou wilt say 'Ay',
And I will take thy word. Yet if thou swear'st,
Thou mayst prove false; at lovers' perjuries
They say, Jove laughs. O gentle Romeo,
If thou dost love, pronounce it faithfully.
Or if thou think'st I am too quickly won,
I'll frown and be perverse and say thee nay,
So thou wilt woo, but else, not for the world.

In truth, fair husband mine, I am too fond,
And therefore thou mayst think my 'havior light.
But trust me, gentleman, I'll prove more true
Than those that have more cunning to be strange.
I should have been more strange, I must confess,
But that thou overheard'st, ere I was ware,
My true love's passion, therefore pardon me.

ROMEO.
Lady, by yonder blessed moon I swear
That tips with silver all these fruit-tree tops...

JULIET.
O, swear not by the moon, the inconstant moon,
That monthly changes in her circled orb,
Lest that thy love prove likewise variable.

ROMEO.
What shall I swear by?

JULIET.
Do not swear at all!
Or, if thou wilt, swear by thy gracious self,
Which is the god of my idolatry,
And I'll believe thee.

ROMEO.
If my heart's dear love...

JULIET.
Well then do not swear!

Pause.

ROMEO.
O, wilt thou leave me so unsatisfied?

JULIET.
What satisfaction canst thou have tonight?

ROMEO.
The exchange of thy love's faithful vow for mine!

JULIET.
I gave thee mine before thou didst request it,
And yet I would it were to give again.

ROMEO.

Wouldst thou withdraw it? For what purpose, love?

JULIET.

But to be frank, and give it thee again.
And yet I wish but for the thing I have,
My bounty is as boundless as the sea,
My love as deep, the more I give to thee,
The more I have, for both are infinite.
All my fortunes at thy foot I lay,
And follow thee, my lord, throughout the world.
Now tell me, what dost thou see?

ROMEO.

I see my Juliet. My sun, my star.

JULIET.

Let that sun shine and show us as we are.
That time of year thou mayst in us behold,
When yellow leaves, or none, or few do hang
Upon those boughs which shake against the cold,
Bare ruined choirs, where once the sweet birds sang.
In me thou seest the twilight of such day,
As after sunset fadeth in the west,
Which by and by black night doth take away.

ROMEO.

To me, fair friend, you never can be old,
For as you were when first your eye I eyed,
Such seems your beauty still.

JULIET.

And how is that?

ROMEO.

Such as would make a man sing like a bird!
Our love was new, and then but in the spring,
When I was wont to greet it with my lays.
Dost thou remember how I used to sing?

JULIET.

I do, my love. And how we used to laugh.

ROMEO.

I'll sing again, and make thy young face smile.

For still I say: to me, thou art so young,
So fair, so touched by nature's kiss
That my breath catches when I look on thee.
I see in thee all time in this one time
Past, present, future, held in thee at once.
Memories and hopes, ay, dreams and fears too,
The universe I see when I see you.

JULIET.

Such words thy used when first thou wooed me, love,
But change is nature, time moves all things on.
All that was once so loud, so brash and bright
Grown peaceful now. The light upon the sea
No longer burns and blinds but gently fills
This room with loving, joy-filled memory.
Adieu!

JULIET runs off and closes the door behind her. ROMEO
goes and knocks. Waits. JULIET *calls from behind the door.*

A thousand times goodnight!

ROMEO.

A thousand times the worse, to want thy light.
Love goes toward love, as schoolboys from their books,
But love from love, toward school with heavy looks.

He turns away. JULIET *puts her head round the door.*

JULIET.

Hist! Romeo, hist!
Romeo!

ROMEO.

My dear?

JULIET.

I have forgot why I did call thee back.

ROMEO.

Let me stand here till thou remember it.

JULIET.

I shall forget, to have thee still stand there,
Remembering how I love thy company.

ROMEO.

And I'll still stay, to have thee still forget,
Forgetting any other place but this.

He tries to squeeze in the door. She resists.

JULIET.

No, no. I would have thee gone.
Goodnight, goodnight! parting is such sweet sorrow,
That I shall say goodnight till it be morrow.

And again the door closes. ROMEO *throws up his hands.*

ROMEO.

Sleep dwell upon thine eyes, peace in thy breast!
Would I were sleep and peace, so sweet to rest!

Silence. Eventually the door opens and JULIET *appears in
her nightgown.*

JULIET.

O blessed, blessed night. I am afear'd
Being in night, all this is but a dream,
Too flattering-sweet to be substantial.

*She stands aside to let him in and closes the door behind
him. Darkness.*

Scene Two

Early morning. Music and the sea. ROMEO *in the half-light.*

ROMEO.

The grey-eyed morn smiles on the frowning night,
Chequering the eastern clouds with streaks of light,
And flecked darkness like a drunkard reels
From forth day's path and Titan's fiery wheels.
Ay me, sad hours seem long.
Still-waking sleep, that is not what it is!
I know it argues a distemper'd head

So soon to bid good morrow to my bed,
But care keeps his watch in this old man's eye,
And where care lodges, sleep will never lie.
O God I have an ill-divining soul!
These visions, night-sights, that do crowd my mind
Torment me so I'm sure I will run mad.

Behind him, JULIET *dances. Her movements begin
gracefully but as the dance continues become jagged,
painful. She spins faster before collapsing.*

I saw my wife, my Juliet, my love,
And deadly piercing steel pressed to her breast.
This torture should be roar'd in dismal hell!
I saw the wound, I saw it with mine eyes!
A piteous corpse, a bloody piteous corpse.
Pale, pale as ashes, all bedaub'd in blood,
All in gore-blood. I swounded at the sight
And lay there on the ground, drunk with my tears.

Light fades on JULIET.

Our violent delights have violent ends
And in their triumph die, like fire and powder,
Which as they kiss consume.
Methinks I see her now – she is below
As one dead in the bottom of a tomb…

JULIET *enters through the door in her nightgown.*

JULIET.
My love, sweet Romeo. Where hast thou been?

ROMEO.
Madam, an hour before the worshipp'd sun
Peer'd forth the golden window of the east,
A troubled mind drave me to walk abroad.

JULIET.
Many a morning have I seen you here,
With tears augmenting the fresh morning dew.
Adding to clouds more clouds with thy deep sighs.
But all so soon as the all-cheering sun
Should in the furthest east begin to draw

The shady curtains from Aurora's bed,
Away from light steals home my dearest love,
And private in his chamber pens himself,
Shuts up his windows, locks fair daylight out
And makes himself an artificial night.
Black and portentous must this humour prove,
Unless good counsel may the cause remove.
Tell me, what sadness lengthens Romeo's hours?

ROMEO.
What, shall I groan and tell thee?

JULIET.
Your looks are pale and wild, and do import
Some misadventure.

ROMEO.
'Tis nothing, love, but that my mind misgives
Some consequence yet hanging in the stars.
I dreamed a dream tonight...

JULIET.
Be ruled by me, forget to think on it.

ROMEO.
O, teach me how I should forget to think!

JULIET.
By giving liberty unto thy soul.
Come, gentle Romeo, we must have you dance!

ROMEO.
Not I, believe me. You have dancing shoes
With nimble soles, I have a soul of lead
So stakes me to the ground I cannot move.
I am past my dancing days.

JULIET (*trying to lift him up to dance*).
You are a lover; borrow Cupid's wings,
And soar with them above a common bound.

ROMEO.
I am too sore inflicted with these thoughts,
These dreams and visions of unnatural death,

To soar with his light feathers, and so bound,
I cannot bound a pitch above dull woe:
Under death's heavy burden do I sink.

JULIET.
To sink in it, and therefore not allow
Myself, your wife and love, to lift thee out?
Why then you burden me and so you burden love,
Too great oppression for a tender thing.

ROMEO.
Is love a tender thing? It is too rough,
Too rude, too boisterous, and it pricks like thorn.

JULIET.
If love be rough with you, be rough with love,
Prick love for pricking, and you beat love down.

ROMEO.
Let wantons light of heart
Tickle the senseless rushes with their heels,
I'll be a candle-holder, and look on.
The game was ne'er so fair and I am done.
I dreamed a dream, my love, I tell thee true.

JULIET.
O, then, I see Queen Mab hath been with you.
She is the fairies' midwife, and she comes
In shape no bigger than an agate-stone
On the forefinger of an alderman,
Drawn with a team of little atomies
Athwart men's noses as they lie asleep.
Her wagon-spokes made of long spiders' legs,
The cover of the wings of grasshoppers,
The traces of the smallest spider's web,
The collars of the moonshine's watery beams,
Her whip of cricket's bone, the lash of film,
Her wagoner a small grey-coated gnat,
Not so big as a round little worm
Prick'd from the lazy finger of a maid.
Her chariot is an empty hazelnut
Made by the joiner squirrel or old grub,
Time out o' mind the fairies' coachmakers.

And in this state she gallops night by night
Through lovers' brains, and then they dream of love.
O'er courtiers' knees, that dream on curtsies straight,
O'er lawyers' fingers, who straight dream on fees,
O'er ladies' lips, who straight on kisses dream,
Which oft the angry Mab with blisters plagues,
Because their breaths with sweetmeats tainted are.
Sometime she gallops o'er a courtier's nose,
And then dreams he of smelling out a suit,
And sometime comes she with a tithe-pig's tail
Tickling a parson's nose as 'a lies asleep,
Then dreams he of another benefice.
Sometime she driveth o'er a soldier's neck,
And then dreams he of cutting foreign throats,
Of breaches, ambuscadoes, Spanish blades,
Of healths five-fathom deep, and then anon
Drums in his ear, at which he starts and wakes,
And being thus frighted swears a prayer or two
And sleeps again. This is that very Mab.
This is she.

ROMEO (*turning from her*).
   Peace, peace, my Juliet, peace!
   Thou talk'st of nothing.

JULIET.
   True!
   I talk of dreams! Thy fearful, deathful dreams,
   Which are the children of an idle brain,
   Begot of nothing but vain fantasy,
   Which is as thin of substance as the air
   And more inconstant than the wind, who woos
   Even now the frozen bosom of the north,
   And, being anger'd, puffs away from thence,
   Turning his face to the dew-dropping south.
   If we must trust the flattering truth of sleep
   My dreams presage some joyful news at hand.
   My bosom's lord sits lightly on his throne;
   And all this morn an unaccustom'd spirit
   Lifts me above the ground with cheerful thoughts.
   I dreamt my husband came and found me dead –

Strange dream that gives a dead mind leave to think! –
And breathed such life with kisses in my lips,
That I revived, and was an empress.
Ah me! How sweet is love itself possess'd,
When but love's shadows are so rich in joy!
Give me thy hand and no more talk of dreams.

ROMEO (*walking back to her*).
Can I go forward when my heart is here?
Turn back, dull earth, and find thy centre out.

They begin to dance together. Suddenly, JULIET *buckles
over with a groan.* ROMEO *watches as she falls to the
ground. He picks her up and carries her out. The sea
darkens as the light fades.*

Scene Three

ROMEO *and* JULIET *enter. He holds a basket of herbs and
flowers.*

JULIET.
She was the prettiest babe that e'er was seen.
An she had lived for us to see her wed
I'd have my wish.

ROMEO.
I must up-fill this osier cage of ours
With baleful weeds and precious-juiced flowers.

He walks away from her into a different pool of light.

JULIET.
This Lammas Eve would be her birthday night
But now she is with God.
She was too good for me.
'Tis since the earthquake a great many years,
And she was wean'd – I never shall forget it –
Of all the days of the year, upon that day.

For I had then laid wormwood to my dug,
Sitting in the sun under the dovehouse wall
When it did taste the wormwood on the nipple
Of my dug and felt it bitter, pretty fool,
To see it tetchy and fall out with the dug!
And since that time 'tis a great many years,
For then she could stand alone, nay, by the rood,
She could have run and waddled all about,
For even the day before, she broke her brow,
And then my husband, he took up the child.
'Yea,' quoth he, 'dost thou fall upon thy face?
Thou wilt fall backward when thou hast more wit,
Wilt thou not, love?' and, by my holidam,
The pretty wretch left crying and said 'Ay.'
To see, now, how a jest shall come about!
I warrant, an I should live a thousand years,
I never should forget it.

Pause.

The clock struck nine when first I sat for news
And pledged myself remain here till it came.
Now is the sun upon the highmost hill
Of this day's journey, and from nine till twelve
Is three long hours, yet it is still not here.

Pause. As ROMEO *speaks,* JULIET *sits, waiting. She stands.*
She sits again. A sheet of paper appears in her hand. She
looks at it.

ROMEO.
The earth that's nature's mother is her tomb,
What is her burying grave that is her womb,
And from her womb children of divers kind
We sucking on her natural bosom find,
Many for many virtues excellent,
None but for some and yet all different.
O, mickle is the powerful grace that lies
In herbs, plants, stones, and their true qualities,
For nought so vile that on the earth doth live
But to the earth some special good doth give,
Nor aught so good but strain'd from that fair use

Revolts from true birth, stumbling on abuse:
Virtue itself turns vice, being misapplied,
And vice sometimes by action dignified.
Within the infant rind of this small flower
Poison hath residence and medicine power,
For this, being smelt, with that part cheers each part,
Being tasted, slays all senses with the heart.
Two such opposed kings encamp them still
In man as well as herbs, grace and rude will,
And where the worser is predominant,
Full soon the canker death eats up that plant.

JULIET *lets forth a long sigh.* ROMEO *drops his flowers and steps into the darkness, leaving roses scattered across the light.*

JULIET.
A deadly sickness now chills up my veins.
What devil art thou, that dost torment me thus?
This torture should be roar'd in dismal hell:
My body has been feasting with my foe
And on a sudden he hath wounded me.
Now there's no help within wise physic's laws.
To prison, eyes, ne'er look on liberty,
All freedom now forbidden me, all joy.
O Romeo! shall death lie with thy wife?
Shall sick contagion stiffen all my limbs
And all my blood be turned to blackened ash?
Shalt thou look on me and know not thy wife?
Shall I look on thee and know not my love?
And shall I fail thee and our partnered life –
But one, poor one, one poor and loving life,
We two in one, our flesh and blood combined
And cruel death shall soon wrench me from thy grasp.
O, break, my heart! poor bankrupt, break at once!

ROMEO *appears next to her.*

ROMEO.
Happily met, my lady and my wife?

JULIET *turns to face him.*

Poor soul, thy face is much abused with tears.
How doth my lady?
How fares my Juliet?
For nothing can be ill, if she be well.

She hands him the piece of paper. He reads.

Ah, Juliet, then now I share thy grief.
It strains me past the compass of my wits.
Past hope, past cure, past help?

JULIET.
All things that we ordained festival,
Turn from their office to black funeral.

ROMEO.
O me! this sight of death is as a bell,
That warns my old age to a sepulchre.
Can it be true?

JULIET.
Give me thy hand,
One writ with me in sour misfortune's book.

ROMEO.
I'll take thy hand and stand as one with thee.
Love is not love
Which alters when it alteration finds.
O, no it is an ever-fixed mark
That looks on tempests and is never shaken.
I am thy husband.

*He holds her. The hold becomes a dance. He nurses her, her
sickness grows, time moves on. As they dance, he speaks.*

How dost my love? How goes the day with thee?

JULIET.
Why quickly, love,
As all days must with ones as old as we.

ROMEO.
O how shall summer's honey breath hold out,
Against the wrackful siege of batt'ring days,
When rocks impregnable are not so stout,

Nor gates of steel so strong but time decays?
Not brass, nor stone, nor earth, nor boundless sea,
But sad mortality o'ersways their power...

JULIET.
...How with this rage shall beauty hold a plea,
Whose action is no stronger than a flower?

ROMEO.
O time will come and take my love away
And, pale, I cower to think upon that day.
This thought is as a death which cannot choose
But weep to have, that which it fears to lose.

The music and movement fade. JULIET *looks at her husband.*

JULIET.
I know thou wilt entreat me to stand forth
And bear this work of heaven with patience.
And yet I fear
The weight shall be too great for me to bear.

ROMEO.
My love...

JULIET.
Hear me.
I shall not bear it, love, but choose to sleep,
Submitting to that timeless cold embrace,
And ending this unnatural decay.
'Tis better far to sleep, at peace, in love,
Than stretched upon this tortured rack of life.
If, in thy wisdom, thou canst give no help,
Nor no physician cure the sufferings to come,
If thou remember all our happiness past
And if thou loves me, as thou sayst thou dost,
Do thou then call my resolution wise,
And with our hands we'll help it presently.

ROMEO.
Death, that would take thee hence to make me wail,
Ties up my tongue and will not let me speak.

JULIET.

Give me some present counsel, for thou know'st
That no one now can speak of remedy
No one spy hope or peace.

ROMEO.

This is a most unnatural speech, my love,
To talk of helping death and going forth
Before thy time, before thy time is done.
I pray thee hush, no more of this.

JULIET.

Ay, more – for there is still far more to come!
O bid me leap, rather than lose myself,
From off the battlements of yonder tower,
Or walk in thievish ways, or bid me lurk
Where serpents are, chain me with roaring bears,
Things that, to hear them told, have made me tremble,
And I will do it, without fear or doubt,
To die at peace, within the soft enfolds
Of quiet night and of my sweet lord's arms.

ROMEO.

And art thou now resolved to this, my wife?
To choose to die? To choose to leave me here?

JULIET.

Behold:
'Twixt all the fiendish loss to come and I,
A bloody knife, shall play the umpire.
For when this sickly burden gets so great
That my small frame has buckled with the weight
Then must thou lay me down and help me sleep.

ROMEO.

Is it e'en so?
Well then, my love, must thou know this of me:
That when I help thee hence to early sleep,
I will be with thee
As I have ever been
Thy twin, companion, guide and follower.

JULIET.

Thy words are strange, I understand thee not.

ROMEO.

Naught strange, except to live without thy touch.
There is no world beyond thy loving gaze
But purgatory, torture, hell itself.
Thy gentle spirit shall aspire the clouds,
Which too untimely here does scorn the earth,
And ere thy much-beloved trembling soul
Is but a little way above my head,
'Twill stay for mine to keep it company.
How then shall I not go with thee, my love?

JULIET.

Go with me?

ROMEO.

                    Ay!

JULIET.

                    No, love! Thou shalt not die!

ROMEO.

Will every little mouse, every unworthy thing
That lives for ever in heaven then look on thee
And Romeo may not?
More honour and more courtship soon shall live
In carrion flies than Romeo: they may seize
On the white wonder of dear Juliet's hand
And steal immortal blessing from her lips,
But Romeo may not, he is banished.
This shall not be. I will go hence with thee.

JULIET.

Art thou a man? thy form cries out thou art,
Thy tears are womanish, thy wild words denote
The unreasonable fury of a beast.
Thou hast amazed me, wilt thou slay thyself?
And slay thy wife who else lives on in thee,
Consigning me then to a second death!
What, rouse thee, man! Thy Juliet lives in thee!
Thou shalt go on and in thy eye and touch

The light of our love still shall warm this world.
Pray, no more talk of going hence with me.
Come now unto thy love and comfort her.

ROMEO.

Thou cut'st my head off with a golden axe
And smilest upon the stroke that murders me.

JULIET.

Thou murders me if thou dost slay thyself
When life and will are strong within thee still.
Thou shalt remain behind and live and love.

ROMEO.

O teach me how to love without my love!

JULIET.

Tut, man, one fire burns out another's burning,
Turn giddy, and be holp by backward turning.
Take thou some new infection to thy eye,
And the rank poison of the old will die.

ROMEO.

Poison? The sweetest balm that e'er was made.
Shall I go on without thee?

JULIET.

Thou shalt and with an unattainted eye,
Find thou a happier life without this love.
Compare my face with those that soon shall show,
And that will make thee think thy swan a crow.

ROMEO.

When the devout religion of mine eye
Maintains such falsehood, then turn tears to fires,
And these who, often drown'd, could never die,
Transparent heretics, be burnt for liars!
One fairer than my love? The all-seeing sun
Ne'er saw thy match since first the world begun.
Say wouldst thou truly go and have me stay?

JULIET.

Ay. I would truly go and have thee stay.

Pause.

ROMEO.
Then go no further than a wanton's bird;
Who lets it hop a little from her hand,
Like a poor prisoner in his twisted gyves,
And with a silk thread plucks it back again,
So loving-jealous of his liberty.
I wouldst thou were my bird
And I could pluck thee back.

JULIET.
This day's black fate on more days doth depend;
This but begins the woe, others must end.

ROMEO.
O we are fortune's fools.

They sink to the floor. They sing 'O Mistress Mine'.

BOTH.
O mistress mine, where are you roaming?
O stay and hear your true love's coming
That can sing both high and low.
Trip no further, pretty sweeting,
Journeys end in lovers' meeting
Ev'ry wise man's son doth know.
What is love? 'tis not hereafter
Present mirth hath present laughter,
What's to come is still unsure.
In delay there lies no plenty
Then come kiss me, sweet and twenty
Youth's a stuff will not endure.

The lights fade.

Scene Four

ROMEO *and* JULIET *dance, the repeating movements of caring and carrying from the previous scene. As they move, he speaks.*

ROMEO.
How dost my love? How goes the day with thee?

JULIET.

O how shall summer's honey breath hold out,
Against the wrackful siege of batt'ring days?
I sicken, Romeo. I sicken, love.

ROMEO.

O time will come and take my love away!
And pale I cower to think upon that day.
How dost my love? How goes the day with thee?

JULIET.

O how shall summer's honey breath hold out,
Against the wrackful siege of batt'ring days?
I sicken, Romeo. I sicken, love.

ROMEO.

O time will come and take my love away.
And pale I cower to think upon that day.
How dost my love?

JULIET.

I sicken, Romeo, I sicken, love.

ROMEO.

O time will come and take my love away.

JULIET.

O time will come and take my love away.

ROMEO.

O time will come and take my love away.

JULIET.

O time.

ROMEO.

My love.

JULIET.

O time.

ROMEO.

My love.

JULIET.

Away.

ROMEO.
  Away.

JULIET.
  Away.

She falls into his arms. ROMEO *sets the sleeping* JULIET *in the bed and leaves quietly. A moment, then she wakes.*

All things now change them to the contrary:
Our instruments to melancholy bells,
Our wedding cheer to a sad burial feast,
Our solemn hymns to sullen dirges change,
Our bridal flowers serve for a buried corpse.
A corpse? O where's my husband? I did bid him come! O
    me, O me! My love, my only life... What is yond
    gentleman? What's he that follows there that would not
    dance? Go, ask his name!
Ah, I am hurt! Courage – the hurt cannot be much. No, 'tis
    not so deep as a well, nor so wide as a church door; but
    'tis enough, 'twill serve. I am peppered, I warrant, for
    this world. Help me into some house, or I shall faint. A
    plague...

ROMEO *enters and goes to her. She pulls away from him.*

Oh, where's my daughter? I did bid her come,
And now she is with God.
On Lammas Eve at night then was she born.
That was she, marry, I remember it well.
'Tis since the earthquake a great many years;
And she was wean'd – I never shall forget it –
Of all the days of the year, upon that day.
And since that time 'tis a great many years,
For then she could stand alone, nay, by the rood,
She could have run and waddled all about.
For even the day before, she broke her brow,
And then, my husband, you took up the child,
'Yea,' quoth thou, 'dost thou fall upon thy face?
Thou wilt fall backward when thou hast more wit,
Wilt thou not, love?' and, by my holidam,
The pretty wretch left crying and said 'Ay.'
To see, now, how a jest shall come about!

I warrant, an I should live a thousand years,
I never should forget it.
And now she is with God!

ROMEO.

Enough of this. I prithee, hold thy peace.

JULIET.

Yes, husband. Yet I cannot choose but laugh,
To think it should leave crying and say 'Ay.'
And yet, I warrant, it had upon its brow
A bump as big as a young cockerel's stone,
A parlous knock, and it cried bitterly.
'Yea,' quoth my husband, 'fall'st upon thy face?
Thou wilt fall backward when thou comest to age,
Wilt thou not, child?' it stinted and said 'Ay.'

ROMEO.

And stint thou too, I pray thee, love, say I.

JULIET.

Peace, I have done. God mark thee to his grace!
She wast the prettiest babe that e'er was seen!

She collapses, exhausted.

ROMEO.

My wife? Juliet? What, art thou still in tears?
Evermore showering? In one little body
Thou counterfeit'st a bark, a sea, a wind,
For still thine eyes, which I may call the sea,
Do ebb and flow with tears; the bark thy body is,
Sailing in this salt flood; the winds, thy sighs,
Who, raging with thy tears, and they with them,
Without a sudden calm, will overset
Thy tempest-tossed body.

He lifts and carries her to the bed, sets her down.

JULIET.

Doth thou not think me an old murderer,
Now I have stain'd the childhood of our joy?
Where is he? and how doth he? and what says
My conceal'd lord to our cancell'd love?
Does he hide himself?

ROMEO.

    Not I; unless the breath of heartsick groans,
    Mist-like, enfold me from the search of eyes.

JULIET.

    O Romeo, now I do spy a kind of hope.
    My spirits stretched now out upon this rack,
    My skin on fire, my mind besieged by pain,
    This is the time, this the time to sleep.
    My love, if thou canst find me one sweet vial,
    One drop of poison, I would temper it,
    That Juliet should, upon receipt thereof,
    Soon sleep in quiet.

ROMEO.

    I'll help thee hence.
    Now comes the wanton blood up in your cheeks,
    Hie you to sleep, I must another way.

He steps towards the audience and the bed fades away into the distance.

Scene Five

ROMEO.

    O now stand forth, come forth thou fearful man!
    Affliction is enamour'd of thy parts,
    And thou art wedded to calamity.
    Uncomfortable time, why camest thou now
    To murder our solemnity?
    Dry sorrow drinks my blood.
    Thou canst not know of that thou dost not feel
    Wert thou as old as I, Juliet thy love,
    Then mightst thou know, then mightst thou tear thy hair
    And fall upon the ground as I do now
    Taking the measure of an unmade grave.
    'My love, if thou canst find me one sweet vial,
    One drop of poison, I would temper it.

That Juliet should, upon receipt thereof,
Soon sleep in quiet.' O mischief, thou art swift
To enter in the thoughts of desperate men!
I dreamt last night of an apothecary:
In tatter'd weeds, with overwhelming brows.
Meagre were his looks,
Sharp misery had worn him to the bones.
I saw him wretched stand before me then
And in his needy shop a tortoise hung,
An alligator stuff'd, and other skins
Of ill-shaped fishes, and about his shelves
A beggarly account of empty boxes,
Were thinly scatter'd, to make up a show.
O, this same dream foreshadows now my need!
I am become this hopeless poisoner
As I bring to my wife this 'one sweet vial'.
This dram of poison, such soon-speeding gear
As will disperse itself through all the veins
That the life-weary taker may fall dead
And that the trunk may be discharged of breath
As rapidly as hasty powder fired
Doth hurry from the fatal cannon's womb.
Come, cordial and not poison, go with me
To Juliet's tomb, for there must I use thee.

*The small blue bottle appears in his hands, and he turns his
back to the audience.*

Scene Six

*The lights dim as the bed appears in the position of the
Prologue.* ROMEO *steps forward and places the bottle at the
foot of the bed.*

ROMEO.
    Give me the light.
    Thou detestable maw, thou womb of death
    Gorg'd with the dearest morsel of the earth.

Slowly lights rise.

It is the east, and Juliet is the sun.
Arise, fair sun, and kill the envious moon,
Who is already sick and pale with grief,
That thou her maid art far more fair than she.
It is my lady, O, it is my love!
Two of the fairest stars in all the heaven,
Having some business, do entreat her eyes
To twinkle in their spheres till they return.
What if her eyes were there, they in her head?
The brightness of her cheek would shame those stars,
As daylight doth a lamp. Her eyes in heaven
Would through the airy region stream so bright
That birds would sing and think it were not night.

JULIET *awakes.*

JULIET.
I do remember well where we should be.
And here we are. Give me thy hand.

*He goes to her and takes her hand, kneeling next to her on
the bed.*

What must be shall be.

ROMEO.

                    That's a certain text.

JULIET.
Dwell not upon our present woes, my love
But on the years of joy and peace behind.
Let us now lie and rest, for we have need.

*And they lie together and gradually fall asleep. Music.
JULIET wakes. She looks out towards the ocean, then back
at her husband.*

Farewell! God knows when we shall meet again.
Ah, see I swoon – with my own tears made drunk!
I have faint cold fear thrills through my veins,
That almost freezes up the heat of life:
I'll wake him up again to comfort me.
Love! What should he do here?

My fears and dreams are savage-wild,
More fierce and more inexorable far
Than empty tigers or the roaring sea.
What if his mixture does not work at all?
Shall I awake again tomorrow morn?
And if I wake, shall I not be distraught,
Environed still with all these hideous fears?

The sun is beginning to rise.

Once more, the grey-eyed morn.
Then He, that hath the steerage of my course,
Direct my sail. Stand forth, my love.

With a kiss to his forehead, she wakes him.

ROMEO.
Wilt thou be gone? it is not yet near day.
It was the nightingale, and not the lark,
That pierced the fearful hollow of thine ear,
Nightly she sings on yon pomegranate tree.
Believe me, love, it was the nightingale.

JULIET.
It was the lark, the herald of the morn,
No nightingale: look, love, what envious streaks
Do lace the severing clouds in yonder east.
Night's candles are burnt out, and jocund day
Stands tiptoe on the misty mountain tops.
I must be gone.

ROMEO.
Yon light is not daylight, I know it, I:
It is some meteor that the sun exhales,
To be to thee this night a torch-bearer.
Therefore stay yet; thou need'st not to be gone.

JULIET.
I am content, so thou wilt have it so.
I'll say yon grey is not the morning's eye,
'Tis but the pale reflex of Cynthia's brow.
Nor that is not the lark, whose notes do beat
The vaulty heaven so high above our heads.
Let's talk, it is not day.

ROMEO.

It is, it is.
It is the lark that sings so out of tune,
Straining harsh discords and unpleasing sharps.
Some say the lark makes sweet division,
This doth not so, for she divideth us.
Some say the lark and loathed toad change eyes,
O, now I would they had changed voices too!
Since arm from arm that voice doth us affray,
Hunting thee hence with hunt's-up to the day.

JULIET.

I must be gone; more light and light it grows.

ROMEO.

More light and light; more dark and dark our woes!

He picks up the bottle and returns to her side.

JULIET.

Goodnight. Goodnight.

ROMEO.

Sleep dwell upon thine eyes, peace in thy breast.

He brings the bottle to her lips and she drinks.

JULIET.

Farewell, farewell! one kiss, and I'll descend.
Art thou gone so? love, lord, ay, husband, friend!
I must hear from thee every day in the hour,
For in a minute there are many days.
O, by this count I shall be much in years
Ere I again behold my Romeo!

ROMEO.

O think'st thou we shall ever meet again?

JULIET.

I doubt it not; and all these woes shall serve
For sweet discourses in our time to come.
Did my heart love till now? Forswear it, sight.
For I ne'er saw true beauty till this night.

ROMEO.

Adieu, adieu. Parting is…

He trails off as he realises she is dead.

Is it even so? Then I defy you, stars!
Away to heaven respective lenity
And fire-ey'd fury be my conduct now!
Ha! Let me see her: out, alas, she's cold,
Her blood is settled and her joints are stiff,
Life and these lips have now been separated.
Death lies upon her like an untimely frost
Upon the sweetest flower of the field.

Pause. Stands, backs away. Pause.

Can I go forward when my heart is here?
My dismal scene I needs must act alone.
Love give me strength! And strength shall help afford.
Well, Juliet, I'll lie with thee tonight.

Kisses her.

Thy lips are warm.

The sun has begun to rise.

Yea, light? Then I'll be brief.
Is there no pity sitting in the clouds
That sees into the bottom of our grief?
Here's to my love.

He drinks from the bottle. Falls forward over JULIET's *body. Silence.*

Epilogue

After a moment, JULIET *rises, dusts herself off, and walks around the bed.*

JULIET.
A glooming peace this morning with it brings,
The sun, for sorrow, will not show his head.
Give me the light.

Sunlight. A ripple of chatter and laughter. Both ROMEO *and*
JULIET *are suddenly younger than we have known them.*
They are strangers. They notice and circle each other, both
watching from a distance.

ROMEO.
What lady's that which doth enrich the hand of yonder
    knight?
O she doth teach the torches to burn bright!
It seems she hangs upon the cheek of night
Like a rich jewel in an Ethiope's ear,
Beauty too rich for use, for earth too dear!
So shows a snowy dove trooping with crows,
As yonder lady o'er her fellows shows.
The measure done, I'll watch her place of stand,
And, touching hers, make blessed my rude hand.

ROMEO *moves towards her.* JULIET *holds his gaze as he*
circles. Suddenly he reaches out and takes her hand.

If I profane with my unworthiest hand
This holy shrine, the gentle sin is this:
My lips, two blushing pilgrims, ready stand
To smooth that rough touch with a tender kiss.

JULIET.
Good pilgrim, you do wrong your hand too much,
Which mannerly devotion shows in this.
For saints have hands that pilgrims' hands do touch,
And palm to palm is holy palmers' kiss.

ROMEO.
Have not saints lips, and holy palmers too?

JULIET.
Ay, pilgrim, lips that they must use in prayer.

ROMEO.
O, then, dear saint, let lips do what hands do,
They pray, grant thou, lest faith turn to despair.

JULIET.
Saints do not move, though grant for prayers' sake.

ROMEO.

> Then move not, while my prayer's effect I take.
> Thus from my lips, by yours, my sin is purged.

JULIET.

> Then have my lips the sin that they have took.

ROMEO.

> Sin from thy lips? O trespass sweetly urged!
> Give me my sin again.

JULIET.

> You kiss by th' book.

ROMEO.

> O blessed, blessed night! I am afear'd
> Being in night, all this is but a dream,
> Too flattering-sweet to be substantial.

JULIET.

> O blessed, blessed night! I am afear'd
> Being in night, all this is but a dream,
> Too flattering-sweet to be substantial.
> Did my heart love till now? Forswear it, sight.
> For I ne'er saw true beauty till this night.
> Give me thy hand.

She takes his hand and they begin to dance. The sea engulfs them.

The End.

DR JEKYLL AND MR HYDE
David Edgar
Adapted from Robert Louis Stevenson

DRACULA
Liz Lochhead
Adapted from Bram Stoker

EMMA
Martin Millar and Doon MacKichan
Adapted from Jane Austen

FAR FROM THE MADDING CROWD
Mark Healy
Adapted from Thomas Hardy

FAUSTUS
Rupert Goold and Ben Power
After Christopher Marlowe

GREAT EXPECTATIONS
Nick Ormerod and Declan Donnellan
Adapted from Charles Dickens

HANSEL AND GRETEL
Stuart Paterson

HIS DARK MATERIALS
Nicholas Wright
Adapted from Philip Pullman

JANE EYRE
Polly Teale
Adapted from Charlotte Brontë

THE JUNGLE BOOK
Stuart Paterson
Adapted from Rudyard Kipling

KENSUKE'S KINGDOM
Stuart Paterson
Adapted from Michael Morpurgo

KES
Lawrence Till
Adapted from Barry Hines

MADAME BOVARY
Fay Weldon
Adapted from Gustave Flaubert

MARY BARTON
Rona Munro
Adapted from Elizabeth Gaskell

THE MILL ON THE FLOSS
Helen Edmundson
Adapted from George Eliot

NORTHANGER ABBEY
Tim Luscombe
Adapted from Jane Austen

NOUGHTS & CROSSES
Dominic Cooke
Adapted from Malorie Blackman

SIX CHARACTERS IN SEARCH OF AN AUTHOR
Rupert Goold and Ben Power
Adapted from Luigi Pirandello

SLEEPING BEAUTY
Rufus Norris

SUNSET SONG
Alastair Cording
Adapted from Lewis Grassic Gibbon

TREASURE ISLAND
Stuart Paterson
Adapted from Robert Louis Stevenson

WAR AND PEACE
Helen Edmundson
Adapted from Leo Tolstoy

Other Titles from Nick Hern Books

Howard Brenton
BERLIN BERTIE
FAUST – PARTS ONE & TWO *after* Goethe
IN EXTREMIS
NEVER SO GOOD
PAUL

Jez Butterworth
JERUSALEM
MOJO
THE NIGHT HERON
PARLOUR SONG
THE WINTERLING

Alexi Kaye Campbell
APOLOGIA
THE PRIDE

Caryl Churchill
BLUE HEART
CHURCHILL PLAYS: THREE
CHURCHILL PLAYS: FOUR
CHURCHILL: SHORTS
CLOUD NINE
A DREAM PLAY *after* Strindberg
DRUNK ENOUGH TO SAY I LOVE YOU?
FAR AWAY
HOTEL
ICECREAM
LIGHT SHINING IN BUCKINGHAMSHIRE
MAD FOREST
A NUMBER
SEVEN JEWISH CHILDREN
THE SKRIKER
THIS IS A CHAIR
THYESTES *after* Seneca
TRAPS

Liz Lochhead
BLOOD AND ICE
DRACULA *after* Bram Stoker
EDUCATING AGNES ('The School for Wives') *after* Molière
GOOD THINGS
MEDEA *after* Euripides
MISERYGUTS & TARTUFFE *after* Molière
PERFECT DAYS
THEBANS

Owen McCafferty
ANTIGONE *after* Sophocles
CLOSING TIME
DAYS OF WINE AND ROSES *after* JP Miller
MOJO MICKYBO
SCENES FROM THE BIG PICTURE
SHOOT THE CROW

Conor McPherson
DUBLIN CAROL
McPHERSON: FOUR PLAYS
McPHERSON PLAYS: TWO
PORT AUTHORITY
THE SEAFARER
SHINING CITY
THE WEIR

Enda Walsh
BEDBOUND & MISTERMAN
DELIRIUM
DISCO PIGS & SUCKING DUBLIN
THE NEW ELECTRIC BALLROOM
THE SMALL THINGS
THE WALWORTH FARCE

Steve Waters
THE CONTINGENCY PLAN
FAST LABOUR
THE UNTHINKABLE
WORLD MUSIC

A Nick Hern Book

A Tender Thing first published in Great Britain as a paperback original in 2009 by Nick Hern Books Limited, 14 Larden Road, London W3 7ST, in association with the Royal Shakespeare Company

Cover image: Brad Swonetx/zefa/Corbis
Cover typography by RSC Graphic Design
Cover design by Ned Hoste, 2H

Typeset by Nick Hern Books, London
Printed in Great Britain by CPI Bookmarque, Croydon, Surrey

A CIP catalogue record for this book is available from the British Library

ISBN   978 1 84842 082 3